Chillingly Poetic

including

The Life of a Corpse Series

by

Elaine M Monaghan

Copyright © 2015 by Elaine M Monaghan

All rights reserved. This book or any portion thereof may not be reproduced or used in any manner whatsoever without the express written permission of the publisher except for the use of brief quotations in a book review.

ISBN: 978-1-326-16882-7

Contents

1. The Crate
2. Just Another Victim
3. Waiting
4. The Life of a Corpse P1 Aware
5. "Goodnight Sweetheart"
6. My Saviour is the Rain
7. I Looked Into His Eyes
8. The Life of a Corpse P2 The Others
9. Senses
10. I Scream
11. I Did and I Died
12. The Life of a Corpse P3 My Death
13. Expel Your Self
14. I Try So Hard
15. I Cried
16. The Life of a Corpse P4 The Child
17. The Pendulum
18. Watchers
19. The Life of a Corpse P5 Voices
20. My Hunger Awaits
21. As I Watch You Sleep
22. The Life of a Corpse P6 Stolen
23. Condemned
24. Crime of Passion
25. There She Goes
26. The Life of a Corpse P7 Hope
27. The Stalker
28. I'm Sorry
29. Can I
30. The Life of a Corpse P8 The Operation
31. To Kill
32. Death's Delight
33. Hooked
34. The Life of a Corpse P9 Salvation
35. The Guillotine
36. Shh
37. The Hanging Tree
38. The Life of a Corpse P10 The Bond
39. Parasite
40. Time
41. Rainbows, Music and Laughter
42. A Taste of Death

Crammed tight within
This ice cold crate
Bound by hands and feet
I wait.
I struggle to live
To take a breath
My destiny
Is surely death.

Foetus like
I'm curled up tight
Never knowing
Day from night.
Cramped body screaming
Wracked with pain
I wish for death
My mind insane?

Cold creeps in and licks
My face
It stirs me from
My dreaming place.
My body's numb
My heart beats slow
I scream at life
To let me go.

Conscious in a
Dreamlike state
My life succumbs to deaths
Cruel fate.
As mind and body
Give up the fight
Freedom comes
As my soul takes flight.

You held me in a
love embrace
Tracing the knife
across my face.
Down my neck
towards my breast
Round my nipple
across my chest.
Beads of blood
began to seep
You pushed in harder
I began to weep.
You held my mouth
bit my ear
Told me
I had nothing to fear.
You sliced a line down
to my tum
Round my hip
towards my bum.
As tears rolled down
you held me tight
Inner strength gone
I had no fight.
You drew the knife
across my spine
I could hear in the distance
a guttural whine.
You pushed the knife
between shoulder blades
Excruciating pain
then it fades.
I felt the wetness
as blood ran free
Just another victim
in your killing spree.

I awaken from my slumber
Sting of rain against bare skin
Shivering from the cold
My nightmares begin
Bound and gagged I lie here
Hidden, left for dead
Memories of my torture
Fill my mind with dread.

My festered wounds are crawling
With insects deep within
They eat me while I live
And burrow under my skin
My mind screams out in horror
Almost driving me insane
I try to lift my head
Yet my body's wracked with pain.

There's nothing I can do
But look upon the moon
Watching, waiting, hoping
Someone finds me soon
I shed my final tears
And settle to my fate
I try to think of good times
While I lie here and wait.

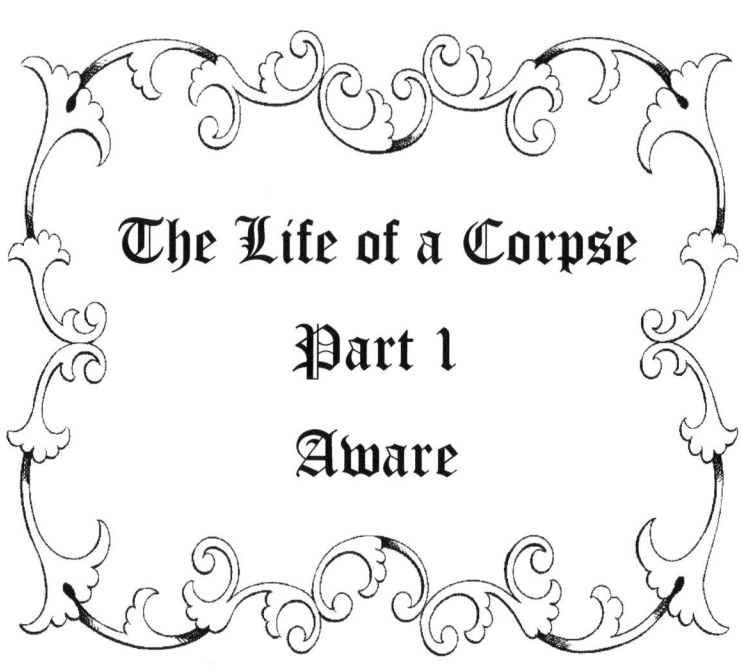

The stars are bright tonight
they seem to mock me where I lie
The full moon looks down on me
from its perch above the sky.

I sense the damp earth beneath me
wet from last night's rain
Sharp stones dig into my back
yet I don't feel any pain.

I'm not sure how long I've been here
day and night merge into one
I only know that time goes by
with the rise and setting sun.

I can't feel my body
but I know my flesh decays
like a rank and putrid apple
that's been left for days and days.

Soon someone will find me
and take me out of here
they'll discover all my secrets
then my death will become clear.

Meanwhile I just lie here
staring at the sky
thinking about what you did to me
and also wondering why.

My heart beats rapid
As a single bead of sweat
Courses its way
From my temple
To my cheek.

My breathing
Becomes laboured
The pain of fear
In my chest is
Almost unbearable.

I lose control of my bladder
Surprised at the shame I feel
My tummy churning
I struggle to contain
The last of my dignity.

My body shakes and
My mind tries to drift
To the safety of darkness
But the sting of your slap
Jolts me back to reality.

You laugh at my weakness
And mock my shame
As you poke and prod
My defenceless body
Tied to this chair.

My pleads for mercy
Do nothing but encourage
You to go on with this
Relentless torture
Of my mind, body and soul.

You yank my head back
Exposing my neck to the
Sharpness of your blade
Cutting deep to release
My life giving blood.

As the warmth and wetness
Flow towards my breast
I smile when I hear you
Whisper in my ear,
"Goodnight Sweetheart".

My Saviour Is the Rain

Splashes of water on my face
Arouse me from my dreams
I lift my head to a nightmare
Hands tied upon high beams
My memories of how I got here
Are still a little unclear
My tortured mind and body
Scream out in pain and fear.
Rain leaks in from the roof
As I try to look around
My naked body dripping
A long way from the ground
Above me the wood is rotting
As rain corrodes the beams
Below me certain death
My destiny it seems.
A calmness overtakes me
As I hear an inner voice
It tells me of my fate
I really have no choice
I know what I have to do
So not to prolong my pain
I struggle to break the beams
And hope my saviour is the rain.

I Looked Into His Eyes

I looked into his eyes and
I saw sorrow, pain and heartache,
I saw misery beyond all
Imagination.

I looked into his eyes and
I saw blood, tears and sweat,
I saw eyes that were pleading for mercy
Screaming for release.

I looked into his eyes and
I saw torment in all its glory,
I saw horror as I'd never seen before
Stare back at me.

I looked into his eyes and
I saw submission and defeat,
I saw acceptance of fate and surely death.
I looked into his eyes and I saw...

Me.

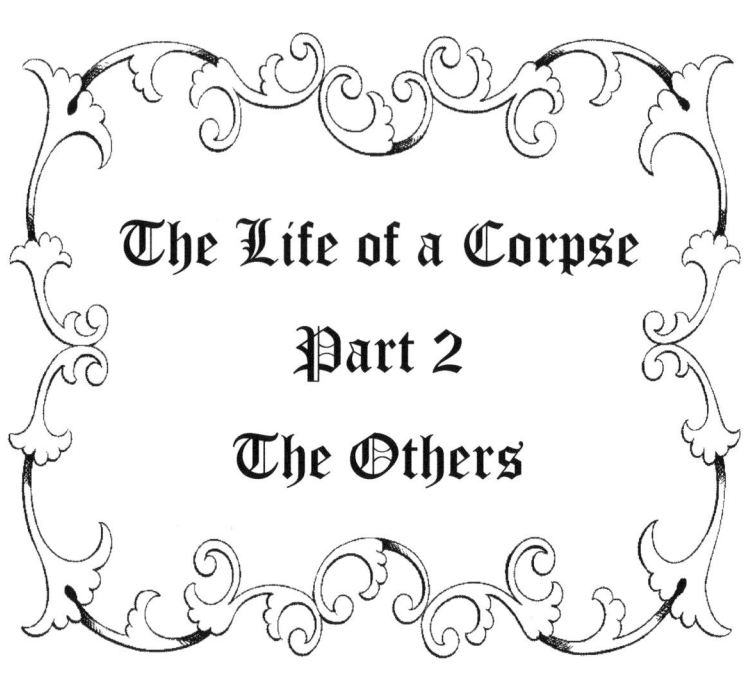

It must have been another month
as the moon is big and full
still no one came to get me
as I lie in my rancid pool.

My flesh is almost gone now
decayed down to the bone
but my mind is still alert
and it knows I'm not alone.

I can sense others around me
almost hear their anguished cry
the frustration and the anger
as they realize where they lie.

I call out to these corpses
hoping they will hear
but all I seem to get returned
is a dreaded sense of fear.

I'll wait a while, till they calm down
and accept their given plight
meanwhile I'll just lie here
and pass another night.

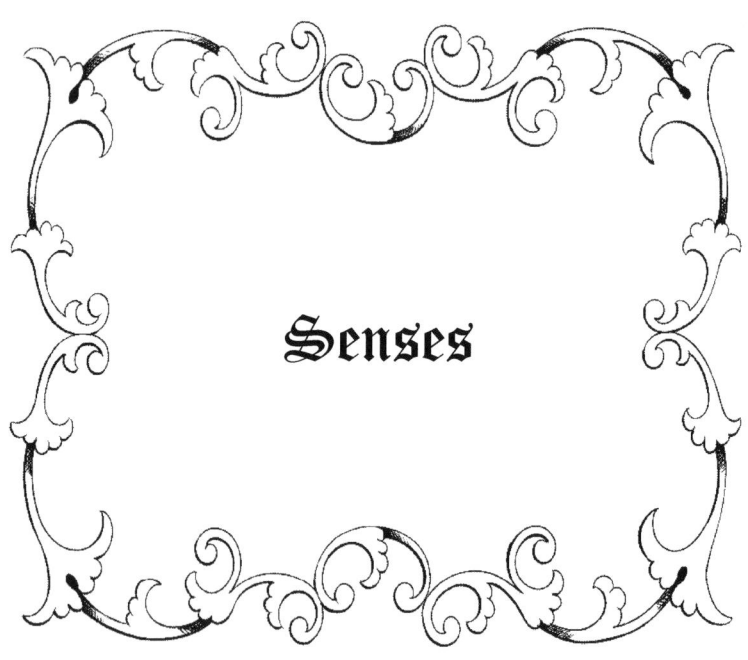

I saw the glint of the knife
As you placed it on my chest
I saw the look upon your face
As you cut across my breast.
I smelt the sweat from your body
As you held me in your grip
I smelt the Devil in your breath
As you kissed me on my lips.
I heard the coldness of your voice
As you whispered in my ear
I heard my heart beat rapid
As you wiped away my tears.
I felt the sharpness of the blade
As you sliced me once again
I felt a rush of blood escape me
As it flowed from severed vein.
I tasted copper in my mouth
As my blood began to flow
I tasted death all around me
As my heart began to slow.
I sense your laughter in the distance
As I start to lose the fight
I sense a darkness overcome me
As I bid this world, Goodnight.

Cold, dark
Body shivering
Teeth rattling
Muscles aching
Realization dawns
I'm buried
Yet alive
I scream
I panic
Can't breathe
Banging, scratching
Splinters, piercing
I'm trapped
No escape
My destiny
To die
After burial?

.

I scream

.

I scream

.

I scream

Approaching from behind
You yanked my head back
Taking advantage of
The strength I lack
A knife you traced
Across my cheek
Cutting ever so slight
My knees went weak
You whispered your venom
To do or I die
No point in struggling
Don't even try
You bit into my ear
Your breath was vile
Acid burned my throat
I could taste my bile
Moving the knife
Just under my chin
You thrust the blade up
Till it pierced my skin
I could feel the edge
Slicing my tongue
I could feel the hot liquid
Enter my lungs
I started to cough
They started to flood
I gasped for breath
And drowned in my blood
I gave you my body
Swallowed my pride
Did what you asked
Yet still.... I died

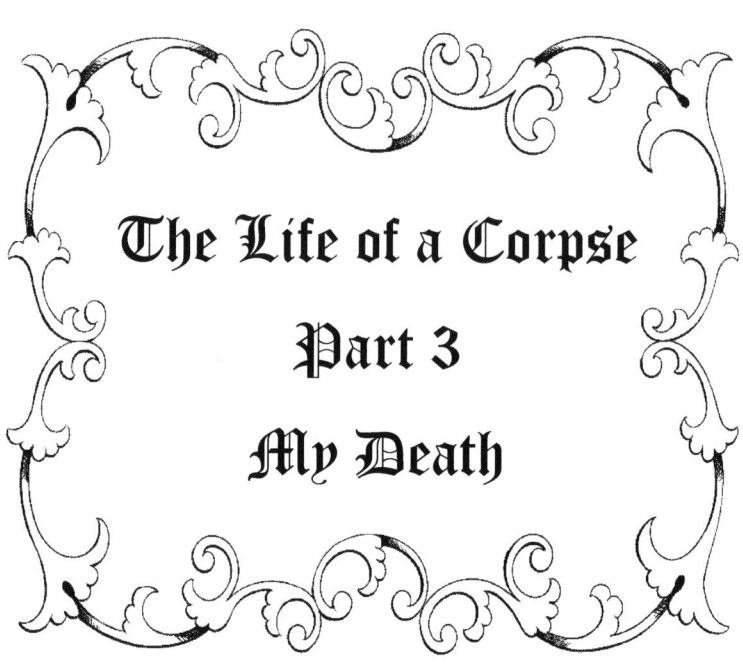

Three more months have come and gone
and the anguished cries have ceased
my flesh has all but gone now
but my thoughts and feelings increased.

I think about the day I died
and the things that happened to me
tied up in a cellar for days on end
wishing he'd set me free.

He tortured me and burned me
he cut me with a blade
he opened up my tummy
my intestines he out laid.

Throughout this he kept me alive
and relished in my pain
he ate a piece of my liver
the act that drove me insane.

He killed me then he dumped me
and here is where I lie
five long months of torture
just staring at the sky.

Expel Yourself

Slice a knife across your arm
Release the darkness from severed vein
Let red flow from the cut
Feel the pleasure of your pain.

Drink blood wine from your palm
Drown the demons in your soul
Taste the nectar of your life
Allow your mind to gain control.

Rip flesh from bone and sinew
Cast the hatred that breeds within
Consume the meat the devil spawned
Free your body of your sins.

Stick your fingers down your throat
Spew the evil from your gut
Rid the sickness from your heart
Cleanse your mind of all the hurt.

Fuck your body with an object
Scream profanities in Satan's name
Reveal the madness that engulfs you
Drive the devil hence he came.

You grab me by the hair
Dragging me back, punching
At my face and body
Forcing me to the ground
Yet I try so hard to fight.

You push my face down
Into the cold wet mud
Ripping at my clothes
Tearing at my skin
Yet I try so hard to fight.

You prise my legs apart
Thrusting your body against mine
Slamming your erection again and again
Deep, deeper into my soul
Yet I try so hard to fight.

You expel your vile seed
Tensing your foul body as you
Pull my hair till my neck feels
Like its about to snap
Yet I try so hard to fight.

You leave me lying in
This cold wet ground
My body weak and bleeding
My mind torn and scarred
Yet still, I try so hard to fight.

I Cried

I cried
Tears of pain
Of sorrow, anguish
And misery
You ignored them.

I lied
Told you what you wanted to hear
Told you I love you
That I wanted you
You didn't believe me.

I denied
You could ever harm me
Or hurt me
Because you loved me
I was wrong.

I tried
So hard to save myself
Begging for my life
Pleading for mercy
Yet you refused.

I relied
On your compassion
The swiftness of the knife
Your knowledge
Again I was wrong.

I died
In your arms
A slow painful death yet
As your tears diluted my blood
I forgave you.

The moon has come and gone again
and snow falls to the ground
it covers me like a blanket
this winter I won't be found.

I've made friends with my comrades
nine of us lie here
we pass time telling stories
our deaths becoming clear.

A child is here, a little girl
she cries out for her dad
the bad man came and took her
snatched from the life she had.

He locked her in the cellar
her hands and feet he bound
made her do such awful things
then committed her body to the ground.

She cries out for her mamma
her anguish and distress
we try our best to console her
but her mind is such a mess.

Meanwhile I just lie here
and listen to her cry
the snow is getting deeper
a blanket from the sky.

The Pendulum

The pendulum swings
Ever closer
Ever nearer
The razor sharp blade
Flashing with every stroke
Ever closer
Ever nearer
I struggle to free myself
From the chains that
Hold me
Still, the pendulum swings
Back and forth
Back and forth
Ever closer
Ever nearer
Slice
I scream
Slice
Blood spurts
Slice
Intestines spew

Slice

Slice

Slice

Watchers

I see you watching
You think I don't know
Your pathetic the lot of you
I wish you would go.

Go back to your lives
And set me free
Of your staring eyes
Stop looking at me.

Don't shed a tear
It won't do me good
Go home to your loved ones
Stop being so rude.

Take your children away
From these awful scenes
What life will they have?
If I'm in their dreams.

Stop soiling your minds
With my bodies debris
I wish you could hear
My final death plea.

The Life of a Corpse

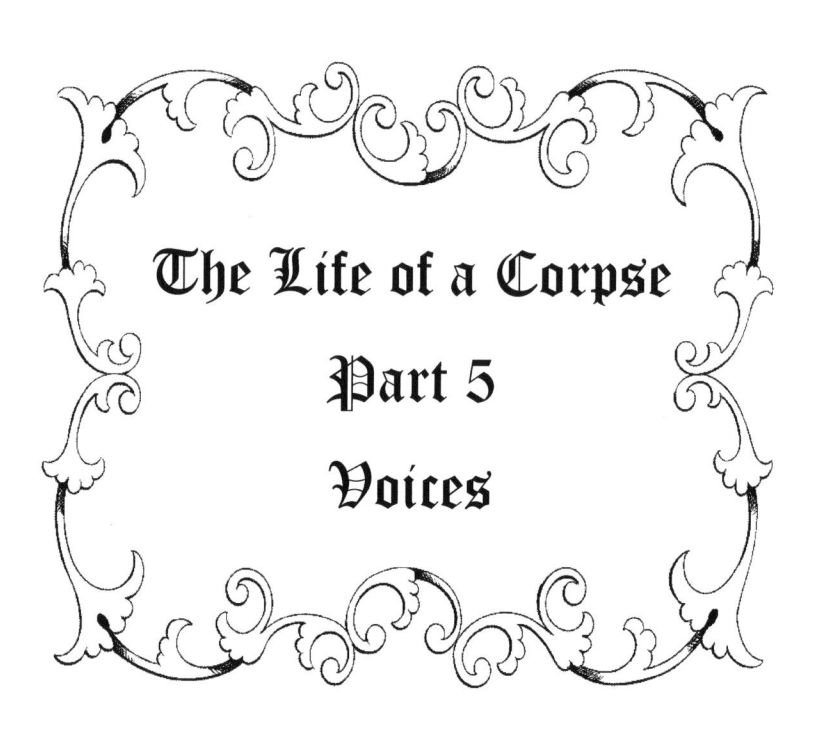

Part 5

Voices

Springtime is approaching
as the snow begins to melt
I feel quite settled lying here
accepting the fate I'm dealt.

Becoming part of the earth
as nature did intend
succumbing to my downfall
my awful gruesome end.

The little girl is quiet now
she doesn't make a sound
she sleeps for all eternity
in this godforsaken ground.

I hear someone approaching
footsteps up ahead
surely not another corpse
there's already ten of us dead.

Voices I can hear
there must be more than one
and laughter in the distance
people having fun.

Their getting so much closer
almost standing on my bones
why can't they see us
or hear our troubled moans.

Alas, they have gone now
I hope they come back soon
meanwhile I just lie here
cursing the crescent moon.

My Hunger Awaits

Shall I let you live
My dear
So I can feast
Upon your fear,
I'll savour the flavour
Of this gourmet delight
If I let you live
Another night.

Or shall I gorge upon
Your death
To steal a drink
From your last breath,
I'll quench my thirst
With fine blood wine
The taste of death
Is so divine.

Maybe I'll let
You decide
To live with fear
Or die with pride
Either way
Doesn't matter to me
My hunger awaits
Your bargaining plea.

As I Watch You Sleep

I sigh and wonder
How this came to be
What do you want?
Or expect from me?
I gave you my all
What more do you need?
Except my life which
I'm willing to concede.
You torture me so
With words more than pain
I never cry out
Nor ever complain
When you bring back those girls
For your sadistic pleasure
You make me watch
While you kill them at leisure.
I clean up your mess
As you sleep content
I wish you would kill me
To end my torment
I've forgotten a life
Without any fears
You held me captive
For eighteen years .
I am free to go
Just walk out the door
Yet as I watch you sleep
I love you more.

The Life of a Corpse

Part 6

Stolen

A year has passed yet still I lie
amid this makeshift grave
to be exposed and put to rest
is a sanctuary I crave.

To be alone among the others
is a thought I cannot bear
so I listen to their stories
the heartache we compare.

A teenage girl has joined us
screaming of her plight
she mourns the death of another
taken from her that night.

The carving knife he showed her
then looked at her and smiled
he ripped her belly open
and stole her unborn child.

He placed its lifeless body
upon her milk-less breast
her little boy just lying there
her little child at rest.

He keeps it as a trophy
which adds to her despair
meanwhile I just lie here
in this unforgiving lair.

Condemned

I'm paraded through the street
While you spit at my face
Your chants echoing in my ears,
Your children throw stones yet
You do nothing to stop them.
I fail to understand
Why my death entertains you so
What joy do you get
From watching a person suffer?
Are you not as guilty?
You condemn me for witchcraft
Yet all I did was heal the sick
Save your husbands
And deliver your children
To your arms in birth.
I laugh at your ignorance
While you mock my demise
Taunting me as I pass you by
Yet I feel sorry for you,
You know not what you do.
Head bowed I'm led
Towards the pile of dry wood
Silhouetted against the night sky
You sing and dance as I'm tied to the stake
Dry grass and tinder placed at my feet.
As the flames consume my body
I hear you gasp and watch
While you clasp your child to your buxom
My screams of pain make you recoil
Yet you stay, unable to avert your eyes.
The acrid smell of my burning flesh
Lingers in the air making you wretch
Tears fall from your eyes
Though you cry not for me
But for the sight you behold.
My pain subsides and my body
Becomes weak and blackened
Yet defiantly I lift my head to see
A look of shame and guilt on your face
It makes me smile before I die.

Crime of Passion

I loved him
Yet he couldn't see
He didn't need that bitch
He needed me.

I'd take care of him
We were meant for each other
He was mine
We belonged together.

Yet he looked at me
With hatred in his eyes
I couldn't stand
That look of despise.

I took out my knife
And cut out his heart
Together forever
Never apart.

It wasn't my intention
To move in for the kill
Yet if I can't have him
No one will.

There She Goes

There she goes
moving her body
swinging her hips
who does she think she is
it's just one big come on
to all those guys
watching her
dance.

There she goes
throwing back the alcohol
laughing and flirting
teasing the barman
flashing her thighs
to all the guys
watching her
laugh.

There she goes
staggering out the door
alone this time
walking home
on her own
where are the guys
that keep her
safe.

There she goes
screaming and kicking
covered in blood
she fights well
yet no match for me
no more dancing
flirting or laughing
there she goes.

The Life of a Corpse

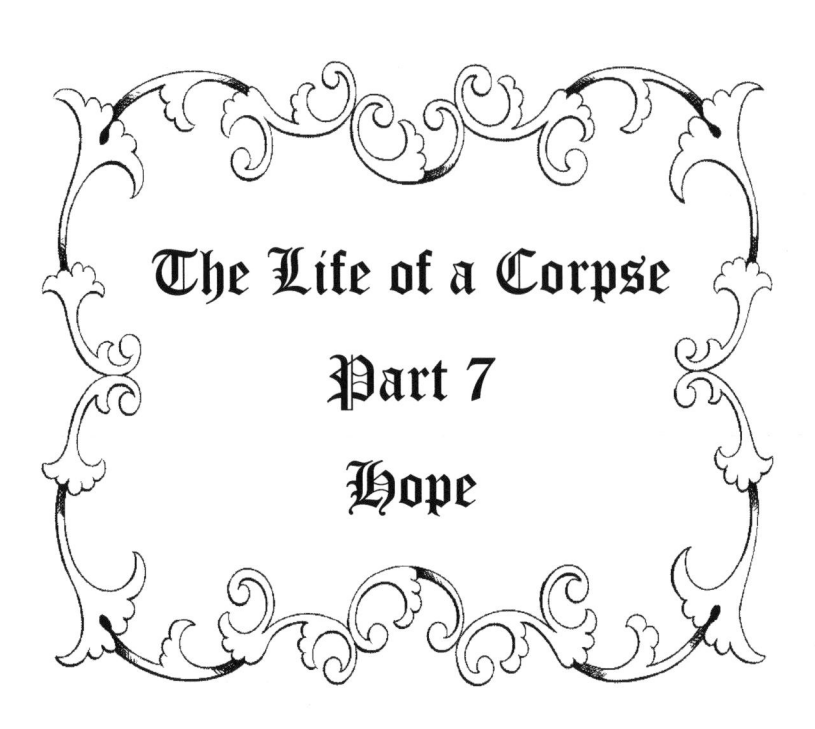

Part 7

Hope

The summer sun beats down on us
from its mantle in the sky
life goes on despite our pain
and no one hears us cry.

People pass by unaware
what lies beneath their feet
until were taken from this pit
our deaths are incomplete.

I awaken from my slumber
to the sound of rustling leaves
a dog comes running, looking
for the ball that he retrieves.

Instead he finds a bone
a prize he cant resist
he returns it to his owner
surely now, we must exist.

Happiness overwhelms us
at the thought of being found
laughter replaces the anguish
in this, unhallowed ground.

Darkness once again returns
another day has passed
meanwhile I will lie here
hoping its my last.

The Stalker

I watched you, as you slept
Soundly in your bed
Watched as you breathed deep
What dreams were in your head?
Did you dream of me? No
You didn't know I was here
Your were unaware that every night
I was lurking somewhere near.
I followed you from afar
And watched your every move
I saw you out the other night
With a man I disapprove
He was using you, why can't you see
He shared another's bed
But don't worry he won't be back
Now that he is dead.
Relax my dear don't thrash about
Everything is fine
I won't harm my precious girl
Now that you are mine
You will be mine, won't you?
We'll live a happy life
We'll move away somewhere quiet
And live as man and wife.
Come! Let me wipe away
The single tear you shed
You'll feel much better leaving behind
The past life that you led
I'll remove the bonds that hold you tight
If you promise to be good
No don't do that, please don't
I thought you understood.
Now look what you did I'm bleeding now
Give me back my knife
Please don't cut me any more
You're supposed to be my wife
Stop it! You're hurting me
Why do you betray
Please don't do this to me
My world is turning grey.

I'm Sorry

Come closer
Don't be scared it's ok
A little nearer
That's it walk this way.

Aw honey don't cry
I won't hurt you, you'll see
Please stop struggling
Lay down quiet for me.

No don't scream
There's nothing to fear
Why won't you stop?
No one can hear.

That's better, See!
It's not so bad
Now don't push me away
Or you'll make me mad.

Ah shit! Now look what I did
I didn't mean to cut you
I'm sorry baby
I didn't mean to hurt you.

Damn it girl
Don't make me cry
Try to stay awake
Please! Don't die.

Can I

Can I take you in my arms
and lay you down upon the floor?
Can I kiss your naked body
then fuck you hard just like a whore?

Can I treat you like an object
to do with as I please?
Can I make you ask for mercy
while you beg upon your knees?

Can I ask you to forgive me
as I relish in your pain?
Can I look upon your face
when I drive your mind insane?

Can I put my hands around your throat
and choke you till you fade?
Can I hold you in my arms
while I cut you with my blade?

Can I watch your blood run freely…
feel its warmth upon my skin?
Can I kiss away your tears
as your death becomes my sin?

Can I?

The Life of a Corpse

Part 8

The Operation

Two more days have passed us by
but still, no one comes near
elation turns to sorrow
and laughter turns to fear.

We start to give up hope again
and settle to our fate
unsure how long we'll be here
our stories we relate.

A middle aged woman's destiny
to be impaled on a wooden stake
while he performed an operation
as she lay there wide awake.

He opened up her chest
her ribs he pried apart
he madly laughed out loud
as he watched her beating heart.

He held it in his hands
and relished in its heat
then ripped it from her body
when it echoed its last beat

Silence overcomes us
as we contemplate her doom
meanwhile I just lie here
staring at the moon.

To Kill

Such a feeling of power
When you put up a fight
My sexual arousal as you
Yield to your plight.

The tears that you shed
As you plead for your life
The fear in your face
When I show you the knife.

The feel of the blade
As it slices your skin
The liquid of life
Pouring out from within.

The sweet smell of blood as it
Runs down your breast
The look in your eyes
When you take your last breath.

The way you relax
Is a sight to behold
As the warmth of your body
Slowly turns cold.

These are the things
That spur me on
Your death feeds my soul
My life is reborn.

Deaths Delight

I trace a smile across your neck
Watch beads of blood flow free
Tears caress your cheeks
Tonight you'll die for me.

I take you in my arms
Whisper in your ear
"Relax my darling, don't you cry
Death will soon be here".

You look at me with pleading eyes
While I run the knife across your chest
A shiver courses through my spine
As blood spills from your breast.

I taste the copper on my lips
My hunger yearns for more
An urge to taste your flesh
Grips me to the core.

I slice the blade toward your groin
Feel a stirring deep inside
I close my eyes in ecstasy
As your screams of pain subside.

I plunge the knife in deeper
Feel your body thrash and spasm
Your death becomes my pleasure
As I delight in my orgasm.

Hooked

I lift my head from drug induced sleep
Disorientated, confused
Where am I?
My head is pounding
Something's wrong
Slowly the mist clears
Blurred eyes begin to focus
Why am I suspended?
In mid-air!
Fear grips me like a vice
I panic, I struggle,
I scream in agony
Pain, so much pain
My back, arms and legs
I turn my head in horror
Hooks piercing my muscles
Ripping my flesh
From bone and sinew
New pain courses through my body
As my heart gives up the struggle
darkness brings relief as I drift
to a death induced sleep.

The Life of a Corpse
Part 9
Salvation

As dawns first light approaches
I hear a distant sound
footsteps are approaching
have we finally been found.

Flashlights all around us
then someone shouts "they're here"
confusion and anxiety
mixes with our fear.

Two long years a secret
waiting our salvation
hidden from the world
like a discarded amputation.

Joy returns and laughter sounds
among my motley crew
we celebrate our finding
amid the morning dew.

Thirteen in all, we lie here
tortured till we died
thirteen peoples future
condemned and then denied.

Meanwhile I just lie here
laughing at the moon
while cautiously and carefully
our bodies they exhume.

The Guillotine

My hands are tied behind my back
A hood placed over my head
I kneel before the guillotine
Soon I will be dead.

I can hear the baying crowds
They laugh and taunt and jeer
My head is thrust between the blocks
As I shed a single tear.

A priest performs my sacred rites
Anointing me with oil
Praying for salvation
An end to this turmoil.

I try to plead my innocence
Yet no one seems to care
I scream for God to save me
A final wretched prayer.

My executioner steps forward
Says his final piece
A gasp erupts among the crowd
The lever is released.

I hear the screech of metal
It bears down on my neck
For a moment I'm left to wonder
Why my head lies on the deck.

Shh

Shh I can hear him
He's coming
Got to be quiet
Hold my breath
Can he hear my heart beat?
Shit he's close
I can smell him
Can he smell me?
Can he see me?
I can see him
Stop shaking
Don't move
Don't breathe
He's passed by
Has he gone?
I think he has
Can't hear him
Have to get out of here
Scared to move
Go slow
No noise
Where is he?
There's a door
Got to make a run for it
Can't see him
Go!

Shit!

He's behind me
Run
Faster
Faster
Almost there

Fuck!!

The Hanging Tree

A distant burning cross
And rows of people dressed in white
Cone shaped hoods with blackened eyes
Light up the fiery night.

Chanting words from text of past
Condemning me to die
For the colour of my skin reflects
The hue of darkened sky.

They draw my blood and seal my fate
To die by twine and noose
And any man shall follow me
If they dare to cut me loose.

I hang here on the old oak tree
As people pass me by
My death! The result of looking
A white man in the eye.

The Life of a Corpse
Part 10
The Bond

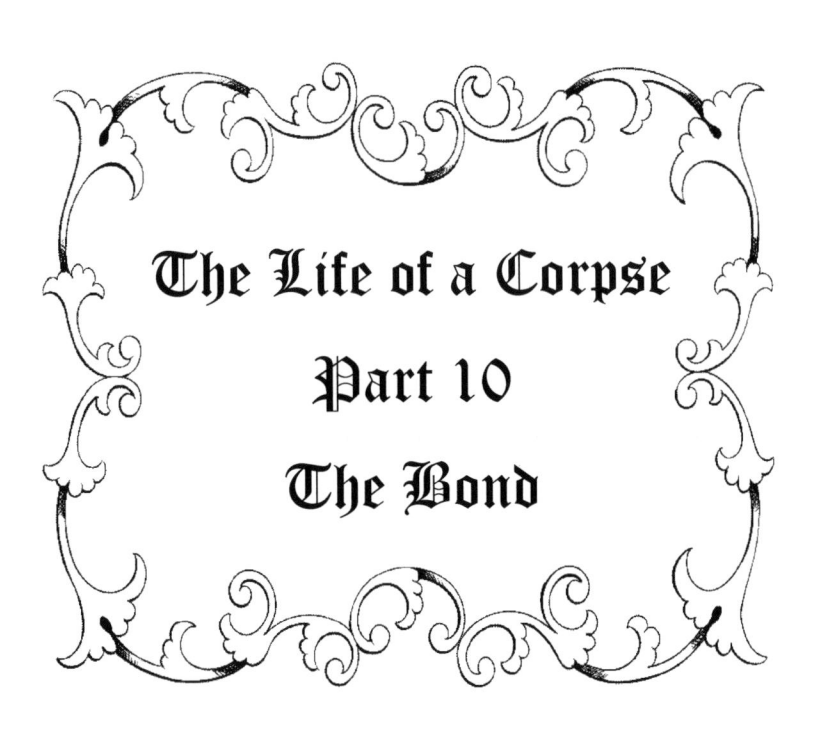

Three long months have passed
since our bodies were exposed
coroner results are published
and cause of death disclosed.

Released back to our loved ones
for them to say goodbye
but our spirits will not settle
however much we try.

We still call out to each other
bonded by our fate
bonded by the two long years
we lay there full of hate.

Our hearts cry out for justice
our souls to be released
our spirits to go on
till we find the heartless beast.

Meanwhile I just lie here
interred within my tomb
surrounded in total darkness
and missing my friend, the moon.

Parasite

It moves inside me
This parasite
Desperate to be released
I feel it scratching
Trying to claw its way out
The devils spawn
Grows with renewed intensity
Waiting to be born
The crawling sensation
Repulses me
I repulse it
It hates me
Burning fire in my throat
Agonising pain in my ribs
This thing forced inside me
Forbids me sleep
Denies me nourishment
Drains the life
From my very soul
Its time
For this rape child
To be born
Searing pain
I scream
My flesh rips
I scream
Blood flows
I scream
Its free
Tears flow

As I cradle my innocent child.

Time

Time means everything, yet
Time means nothing.
I am time
because time means all to you.
Time is precious
because you have none.
Time is all
Time is nothing
I take time
Away.
I am time
all the time you have
Belongs to me.
Don't look at the clock
it tells lies.
Your time is mine
My time is infinite
My time is when I say.
My time is
Whenever
I say, yet
I let you enjoy
I let you cry
I let you be.
You belong to me
don't you?
Yes! You do
because I am time
No one surpasses time!!!
Do they?
.
.

Do they???

Rainbows
Music
And Laughter

I see a rainbow in the distance
Its colours so intense
It's trying to take away from me
A darkness so immense,
It reaches out toward me
Trying to draw me near
Yet the darkness wants to keep me
To fill my life with fear.

I hear music in the distance
It sounds so sweet and good
It's trying to take away from me
A dullness in my mood,
It reaches out toward me
And tries to enter my head
Yet the dullness wants to keep me
To fill my mind with dread.

I hear laughter in the distance
Like music to my ears
It's trying to take away from me
My sorrow and my fears
It reaches out towards me
And tries to lift my soul
Yet the sorrow wants to keep me
With my sanity, its goal.

I see you in the distance
Urging me to follow
You're trying to take away from me
The darkness and the sorrow
You reach out towards me
And hold me in embrace
My insanity and fears
Leave without a trace.

A Taste Of Death

The warm air wakens me
From this cold slumber
Raised from my sleep
In a dreamlike state
I tremble at your touch.

You peel away the cloth
That adorns my naked body
I feel the warmth of your fingers
As you hold me in your hands
Caressing my pallid skin.

You breathe deeply
Inhaling my sweet aroma
Your heart beats rapid
As you reach for the knife
That will pierce my tender flesh.

I feel the sharpness of the blade
As you slice it through my skin
I scream, yet silence
You lay me down on a soft bed
Placing a blanket to hide my nakedness.

You lift me to your lips
Gently kissing me
Licking me with your tongue
I bid goodbye to this world
As you bite into…

Your cheese sandwich.

Printed in Great Britain
by Amazon